Stuck on Cactus

AMERICAN DESERT LIFE

Library of Congress Cataloging-in-Publication Data

Morrison, Yvonne.
  Stuck on cactus : American desert life / by Yvonne Morrison.
      p. cm. -- (Shockwave)
  Includes index.
  ISBN-10: 0-531-17768-8 (lib. bdg.)
  ISBN-13: 978-0-531-17768-6 (lib. bdg.)
  ISBN-10: 0-531-15497-1 (pbk.)
  ISBN-13: 978-0-531-15497-7 (pbk.)
1. Cactus--Juvenile literature. 2. Cactus--Southwest, New--Juvenile literature.
I. Title. II. Series.

  QK495.C11M587 2008
  583'.56--dc22

2007012243

Published in 2008 by Children's Press, an imprint of Scholastic Inc.,
557 Broadway, New York, New York 10012
www.scholastic.com

SCHOLASTIC, CHILDREN'S PRESS, and associated logos are trademarks
and/or registered trademarks of Scholastic Inc.

08 09 10 11 12 13 14 15 16 17
10 9 8 7 6 5 4 3 2 1

Printed in China through Colorcraft Ltd., Hong Kong

Author: Yvonne Morrison
Educational Consultant: Ian Morrison
Editor: Janine Scott
Designer: Juliet Hughes
Photo Researchers: Jamshed Mistry and Janine Scott
Illustration by: Xiangyi Mo and Jingwen Wang (pp. 30–31)

Photographs by: Big Stock Photo (cutting open prickly pear, p. 26); **Digital Vision**
(p. 3; cactuses in landscape, p. 13; cactus bud, p. 15; prickly pear, p. 28; cactuses,
pp. 32–33); **Getty Images** (cover; fine spines, pp. 14–15; saguaro flower, saguaro
fruits, pp. 22–23; harvesting saguaro fruits, p. 25); **Ignacio Urquiza/Weldon Owen**
(harvesting agave, p. 27); **Jennifer and Brian Lupton** (teenagers, pp. 32–33); **More
Images/NPL** (nesting bird, pp. 14–15); **Photolibrary** (p. 7; cactus garden, pp. 8–9;
coastal cactuses, epiphyte cactus, pp. 10–11; cactus roots, p. 13; p. 14; barbed spines,
p. 15; pp. 16–17; relocating cactus, p. 19; pp. 20–21; pincushion cactus; beavertail
cactus; Brazilian blue cactus, p. 23; cactus fence, cactus spines, pp. 24–25);
Stock.Xchng (p. 34); **Tranz/Corbis** (cactuses in snow, p. 11; cactus, Kew Gardens,
pp. 18–19; nopales stall, pp. 26–27; saguaro skeleton, p. 28; p. 29)

All other illustrations and photographs © Weldon Owen Education Inc.

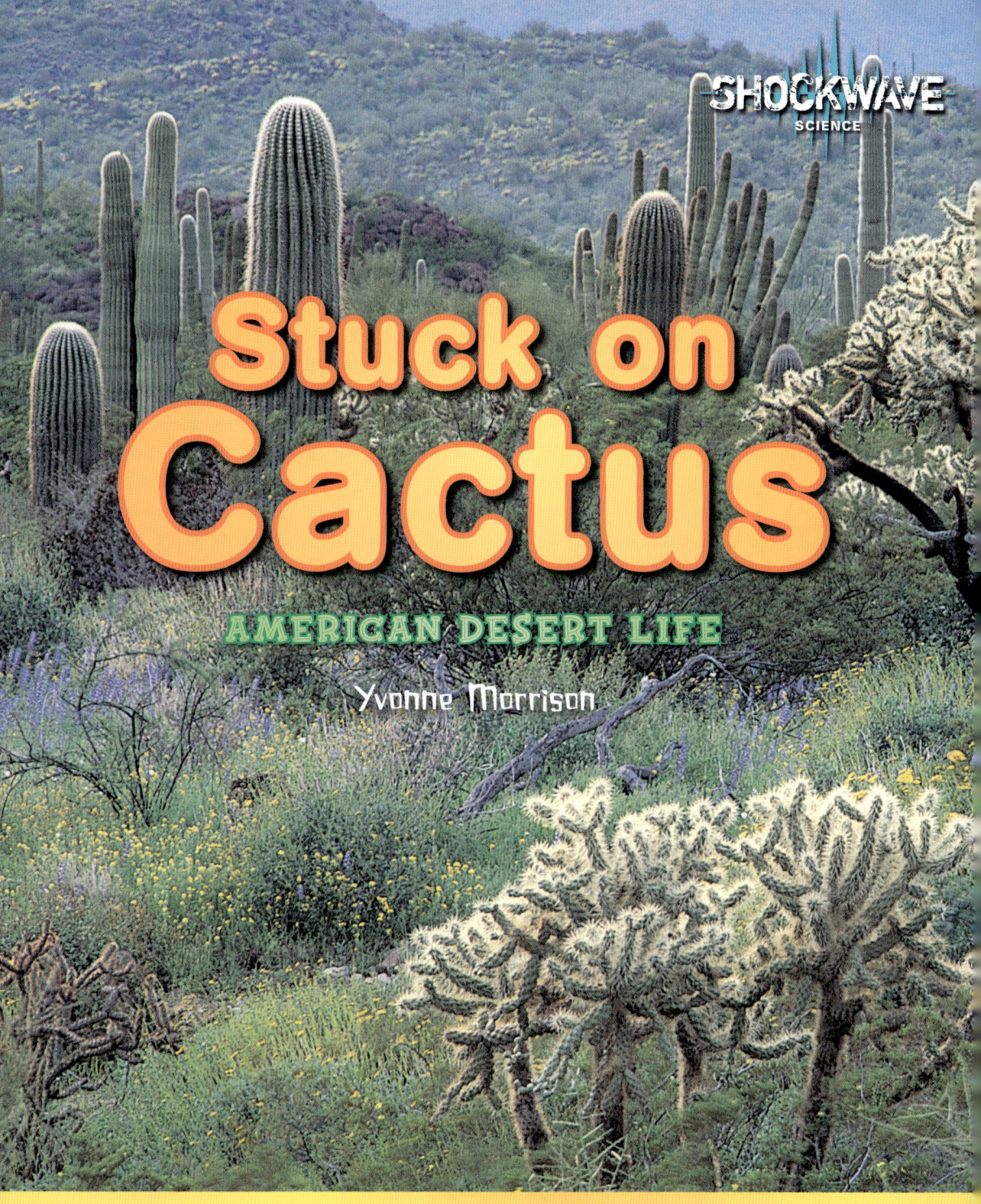

SHOCKWAVE
SCIENCE

Stuck on Cactus

AMERICAN DESERT LIFE

Yvonne Morrison

children's press®

An imprint of Scholastic Inc.

NEW YORK • TORONTO • LONDON • AUCKLAND • SYDNEY
MEXICO CITY • NEW DELHI • HONG KONG
DANBURY, CONNECTICUT

CHECK THESE OUT!

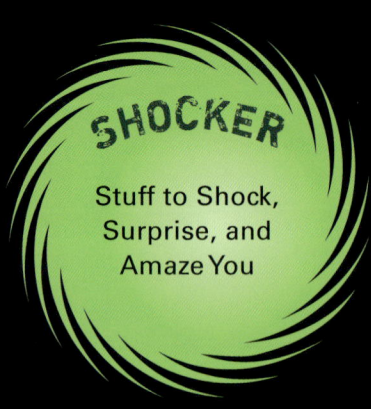

SHOCKER

Stuff to Shock, Surprise, and Amaze You

Quick Recaps and Notable Notes

Word Stunners and Other Oddities

The Heads-Up on Expert Reading

Links to More Information

CONTENTS

areole (*AIR ee ole*) a small lump on a cactus stem that produces leaves, spines, and flowers

cactus (*KAK tuhss*) a water-storing plant that is native to the Americas and usually has clusters of spines

rib a vertical ridge on a cactus stem

species (*SPEE sheez*) a group of plants or animals that share common characteristics and are able to reproduce

spine a modified leaf; usually a stiff, pointed structure growing from an areole

succulent (*SUHK yuh luhnt*) any plant that can store large amounts of water

taproot a large main root of a plant that grows downward

For additional vocabulary, see Glossary on page 34.

The word *species* can be both singular and plural. Other words that can be both include: *sheep, moose, deer,* and *swine*.

When you think of a **cactus**, do you imagine
the tall, spiky plants that you see in Western movies?
In fact, there are about 2,000 different **species**
of cactus. They come in all kinds of bizarre shapes
and sizes. Some are the size of buttons, less than
an inch across. Some are huge, tree-like plants,
up to five stories high. Many have colorful flowers.

Cactuses originally came from North and South
America. Most cactuses live in hot, dry places.
However, some can survive in Alaska and
near Antarctica!

Cactuses have the ability to store water. Fleshy plants with stems that store water are called **succulents**. All cactuses are succulents. However, not all succulents are cactuses.

What Makes a Cactus a Cactus?

Cactuses have thick, fleshy stems. They usually have clusters of **spines**. The spines grow from **areoles**. Areoles are bud-like structures that occur in a regular pattern on the stem.

Water-storing stem

Spines

Areole

9

Cactuses Are Survivors

Cactuses are survivors. Many cactuses grow in **arid** regions. Some of these regions are so dry that it may rain only once every ten years. To survive, the cactuses take the moisture they need from fog, mist, and dew. Cactuses are found mostly from Canada to the tip of South America. Many species live in Mexico and the southwestern United States. Cactuses are also found on the Galápagos Islands, in the southern Pacific Ocean. Some cactuses survive in the Andes Mountains of Peru, at an altitude of 15,000 feet.

Many cactuses grow in rocky and hilly deserts, where they receive small amounts of rainfall. There are also rain-forest species that live in trees. Rain-forest cactuses look very different from desert cactuses. They often have broad, flat stems that look much like leaves. Cactuses that live in rain forests do not need soil.

The heading and first sentence are exactly the same! This makes me think that the text on this page will explain why and how cactuses survive. It sure helps to be able to predict what will be on the page.

West Indies

Some rain-forest cactuses live in the branches of trees. They are **epiphytes**. They get their moisture from the rain, mist, or fog.

Some cactuses can endure varied conditions of long droughts, blazing desert sun, night frosts, and even snow.

11

Moist Miniatures and Juicy Giants

Cactuses are like storage tanks. They absorb and store water inside their swollen stems. Some people think that if you cut off the top of a cactus, you will find clear water. However, the moisture is actually contained in **cells**, held like water in a sponge.

Cactuses are often shaped like globes. This is a shape that can hold a lot of water. Many cactuses have stems with **ribs**. The ribbed stems expand and contract like an accordion. When water is plentiful, they expand. They contract when water is scarce. Cactus skin is tough and waxy. The waxy coating helps prevent water from **evaporating**.

Cross Section of a Cactus Stem

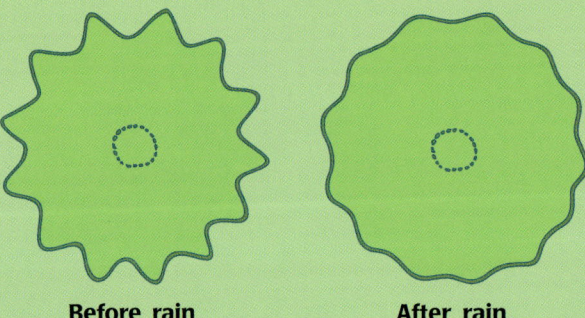

Before rain   **After rain**

The ribs on a stem help the cactus expand without splitting when the stem swells after a rainfall. The ribs also provide shade for parts of the plant.

Many cactuses have long roots. The roots spread out over a large area just below the surface of the ground. This way, they can quickly absorb a large amount of rainwater during a brief downpour. Some cactuses have **taproots**. A taproot is a large root that grows straight down. It has the ability to store large amounts of water. It also helps anchor the plant in the soil.

How Cactuses Hold Water

- act like storage tanks
- globe shape can hold lots of water
- ribbed stems expand and contract
- waxy skin prevents evaporation

Sharp Spines, Furry Spines

Most cactuses have sharp spines. Spines probably evolved from leaves or bud scales. Spines come in many different colors and shapes. They may be arranged in swirls or in lines. Spines have many functions. They provide surfaces on which moisture from the air can **condense**. They channel water to the roots of the cactus. They act like a cocoon around the cactus, keeping it shaded in summer and warm in winter. Low temperatures can harm cactuses. When water inside a cactus freezes, it expands. Sometimes this causes the cactus to burst open. The spines also give the plant some protection from hungry animals.

Some people use the word *cacti* instead of *cactuses*. Both plurals are acceptable. Other words that have more than one plural form include: *formula* (*formulae* or *formulas*) and *octopus* (*octopi* or *octopuses*).

Not all cactuses have spines. The old man cactus has a coat of long, white hair. The hair helps shade it from the harsh desert sun.

CACTUS SPINES

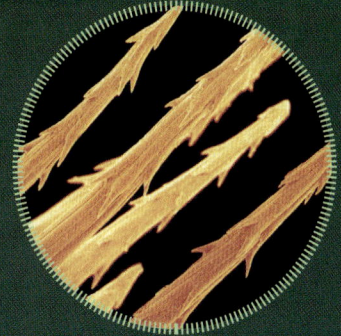

Spines can be painful to touch. They are barbed, like an arrow or a fishhook. The tip of the spine goes into skin easily. It can be difficult to pull out.

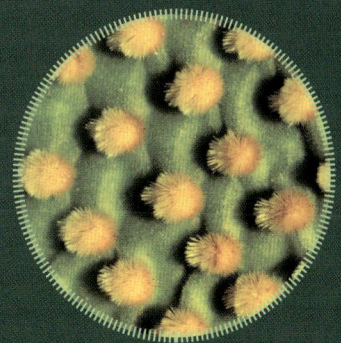

Some spines are very fine. Fine spines that look like fuzz can get stuck in your skin by the hundreds. They need to be removed with tweezers or tape.

All cactuses have growth buds called areoles. Spines, side branches, flowers, and fruit grow from areoles.

SHOCKER

Some cactuses have dagger-like spines that are thick enough to pierce the sole of your shoe and sink deep into your foot.

Spines can prevent a cactus from being eaten. However, they don't stop all animals. Some birds even build their nests on cactuses.

Cactus Flowers

All cactuses produce flowers. The flowers are usually white, orange, red, or yellow. Some are as small as 0.2 inches across. Others are as large as 16 inches across! Cactuses usually flower once a year. Many flowers are short-lived. They bloom for only a few days. Other species of cactus flower for weeks.

During the day, bees and birds drink nectar from the flowers. As they drink, cactus pollen sticks to their bodies. They then transfer this pollen from one flower to another. This is called **pollination**. After this process, the flower wilts and fades. Fruit begins to grow and swell at the flower's base. Seeds grow inside. The seeds are then spread by animals, wind, and even rain. Sometimes the seeds lie under the ground. They wait to sprout when the rains come.

Reproduction
- animals transfer pollen
- flower wilts and fades
- fruit begins to grow
- seeds grow inside fruit
- animals, wind, and rain spread seeds
- new cactuses begin to grow

There are about 450 kinds of cactuses that bloom only at night. They attract bats and moths that feed at night. The saguaro (*suh WAH roh*) cactus blooms only once each year. The flowers last just one night and one day. Some bats come to drink the nectar. They spread pollen as they visit other flowers.

Red and yellow flowers are common among cactuses. These bright colors help attract birds and insects in the daytime. Night-flowering cactuses that need to attract bats and moths produce white flowers.

SHOCKER

Many cactuses have sweet-smelling flowers. The scent attracts insects and birds. However, one kind of cactus has flowers that smell like rotting meat. The smell is attractive to flies.

Usually one flower grows from one areole. At the center of a cactus flower are the stamens. These are the pollen-producing parts of a flower.

Cactus Crazes

In the sixteenth century, explorer Christopher Columbus found melon cactus and prickly pear in the West Indies. He brought some samples back to Queen Isabella of Spain as a gift. In the late eighteenth century, people in Europe became fascinated with "hedgehog plants," as they called cactuses. They couldn't get enough of them. You might say they were stuck on cactuses!

Many explorers made trips across the Atlantic Ocean just to collect new species and bring them to Europe. The English royal family had huge hothouses built for growing cactuses. In England during **Victorian** times, some species of cactus were extremely valuable. However, by the late nineteenth century, plant fashions in Europe changed. People lost interest in cactuses. They started collecting orchids instead. Today, many people are again collecting cactuses.

Kew Gardens

That's helpful! I already know something about Christopher Columbus and Queen Isabella. It is interesting to find them mentioned in a book about cactuses. These kinds of connections make reading easier, and a lot more fun.

Kew Gardens in London has greenhouses with collections of rare plants. The Princess of Wales Conservatory has many cactuses and plants from arid areas.

Some people take cactus plants from the wild and sell them to dealers. An international treaty makes it illegal to collect cactuses from the wild. Instead, growers have to collect seeds and grow new cactuses from scratch. All cactuses are now on the **endangered** list.

In Ecuador, this rare cactus is being relocated to a safer place.

Did You Know?

Destroying or vandalizing a cactus is called cactus plugging. Sometimes the cactus is cut open, drained, filled with explosives, and then blown apart. Sometimes it is shot to pieces. Cactuses are protected under the law, so cactus plugging is illegal. Many of the cactuses people destroy are more than 100 years old!

Desert Giants

In the middle of the Sonoran Desert stand the desert giants. The saguaro cactus can reach a height of 60 feet. They can weigh as much as eight tons and hold hundreds of gallons of water. These amazing plants grow into strange shapes that look almost human.

The giant saguaro starts life as a tiny seed. Most seeds are eaten by birds before they can sprout. Saguaro seedlings that do survive grow very slowly. After their first year, they might be only a quarter-inch tall! Sometimes they get wiped out by flash floods. The luckiest saguaro seedlings live under a "nurse plant." This is a tree that gives them shelter and protection. By the time the nurse plant dies, the saguaro is big enough to survive the conditions.

California
Arizona
Sonoran Desert
MEXICO

Saguaros grow only in southern Arizona, southeastern California, and northwestern Mexico.

Growth of a Saguaro Cactus

150–200 YEARS

100 YEARS

75 YEARS

50 YEARS

10 YEARS

2 inches   12 feet   20 feet   30 feet   50 feet

Woodpecker

Owl

Saguaros provide a home and food source for many desert animals. The male Gila (*HEE luh*) woodpecker pecks out a hollow for his mate. The cactus heals itself by forming wood around the scars. The female lays her eggs inside the hollow. The hollow is cool because it is surrounded by moist cactus flesh. When the Gila woodpecker is finished with its hollow, birds such as owls often move in. When the cactus finally dies, the soft flesh rots away. The hollow, wooden scars are left behind. They are called "saguaro boots." Many small animals, such as lizards and scorpions, use them as nests.

Saguaros grow straight upward into a thick column. When they are about 30 years old, they may begin to produce flowers and fruit. When they are 75 years old, their first arms grow. Saguaros can live to be more than 200 years old.

21

The saguaro cactus blooms in spring, during May and June. The flowers are up to four inches long. The fruit of the saguaro cactus is shaped like an egg. It begins to grow at the base of a flower. A month later, the fruit opens. It is filled with red, sweet flesh and black seeds.

Birds and insects come to eat the fruit and seeds. Some bats eat the fruit too. Coyotes feast on the fallen fruit.

Did You Know?

The saguaro flower is Arizona's state flower. The cactus wren (below) is the state bird.

After many years, the saguaro dies. The flesh begins to rot. Insects, scorpions, spiders, and lizards move in. Finally, all that is left of the saguaro is its woody ribs.

SHOCKER

In 1982, a man shot at a very tall saguaro cactus. Several bullets went through one branch. The heavy branch fell off. It crushed him to death!

CACTUS NAMES

Cactuses have scientific names. Most people use their common names. Common names are often very descriptive. However, they may be as long as the scientific names!

Common name: **Pincushion cactus**
Scientific name: *Mammillaria hahniana*

Common name: **Beavertail cactus**
Scientific name: *Opuntia basilaris*

Common name: **Brazilian blue cactus**
Scientific name: *Pilosocereus glaucescens*

23

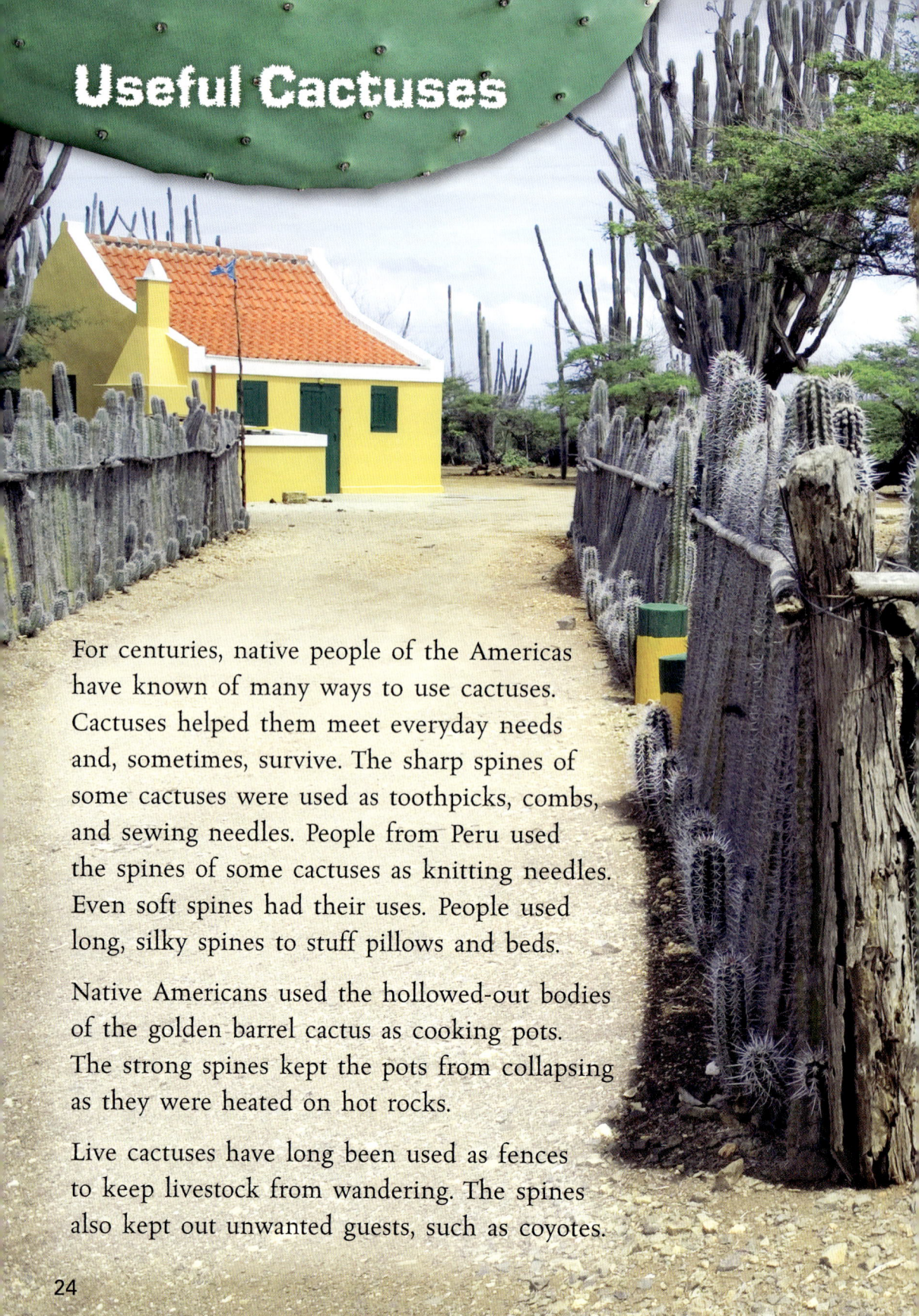

Useful Cactuses

For centuries, native people of the Americas have known of many ways to use cactuses. Cactuses helped them meet everyday needs and, sometimes, survive. The sharp spines of some cactuses were used as toothpicks, combs, and sewing needles. People from Peru used the spines of some cactuses as knitting needles. Even soft spines had their uses. People used long, silky spines to stuff pillows and beds.

Native Americans used the hollowed-out bodies of the golden barrel cactus as cooking pots. The strong spines kept the pots from collapsing as they were heated on hot rocks.

Live cactuses have long been used as fences to keep livestock from wandering. The spines also kept out unwanted guests, such as coyotes.

Some cactuses are a good source of food. Some have even helped people catch fish. The sap of the dagger cactus is **toxic**. Native people crushed the stems and threw them into streams. The stems released toxins that temporarily stunned fish. The fish could then be easily scooped out by hand. The barrel cactus also helped with fishing. Its sharp spines are strong and hook-shaped. They are perfect for making fishhooks.

The Tohono O'odham (*Toh HO no o O dam*) Native Americans harvest the saguaro fruit. They pull the fruit down using long poles. They scoop the flesh into buckets. Then they leave behind the fruit skins as an offering to the gods of rain.

There are some species of cactus that can be safely eaten by humans. However, many others are toxic. Their sap can cause diarrhea and vomiting. There are also other succulents that look like cactuses and are poisonous.

Prickly pear is the cactus most commonly eaten by people. It has flat pads that taste a bit like green beans. They can be prepared like any other vegetable. The pads can also be dried and made into tea. To remove the spines, the pads are scraped with a knife. Usually the harvesters remove the spines before the pads are sold. The pads from the prickly pear are known as nopales (*no* PAH *lays*). They are very popular in Mexico.

The fruit of the prickly pear is very sweet and juicy. This fruit is sometimes called cactus apple or tuna. The fruit has a thick, leathery skin. You can eat it as is. You can make it into a dessert or smoothie. It is also candied and made into jelly. The only problem is that it contains many hard seeds. The seeds must first be removed.

Nopales can be found at markets in Mexico and the United States. Nopales are healthful. They are high in fiber and low in fat. They contain iron, calcium, and vitamins A, B6, C, and K.

The flesh of the agave cactus is used to make a honey-like syrup called agave nectar.

Warning!

Don't eat any cactus or succulent unless you have checked with an expert first. Many cactuses are toxic. They are also very prickly to eat!

cooking pots

fishhooks

medicines

needles — **Cactuses** — fences

weapons

food   personal grooming

Native Americans have used cactuses as medicine for hundreds of years. It is believed that **arthritis** can be treated with cholla cactus. Pads of prickly pear are sliced open and placed on a wound to heal it and relieve pain. The juice of the prickly pear can also soothe insect bites, burns, rashes, and sunburn. Modern scientists are beginning to research the use of cactuses as medicines. Cactus sap is being tested to see if it can help control **diabetes**.

Traditional Remedies From Parts of the Prickly Pear

Native American Groups

Dakota and Pawnee:
• peeled stems used to treat wounds

Lakota:
• cut stems used to treat snakebites

Nanticoke:
• juice of fruit used to treat warts

Prickly pear

The insides of some tall cactuses, such as saguaro, are woody. When these cactuses die, a woody skeleton is left. This wood can be used as firewood, for carving, or for building. The long, straight saguaro ribs can be bent into items such as baskets. You can collect these ribs only with permission from the property owner.

SHOCKER

The prickly pear grows well in the Canary Islands. In just one year, the Canaries produced six million pounds of **cochineal**, made from 400 billion insects!

SEEING RED!

In 1519, Hernando Cortés of Spain invaded Mexico. He was amazed to see the **nobles** dressed in robes dyed a vivid red. Red dyes in Europe at the time were pale and dull.

Cortés soon found out how the dye was made. Cochineal insects live on prickly pear cactuses. The female beetles eat the red cactus berries. The red color stays in their bodies. These beetles are killed. They are dried in the sun and then crushed. This makes a dark red powder called cochineal.

Cortés sent the powder back to Spain. It quickly became popular. People began to set up prickly-pear farms so that they could farm the tiny beetles. In 1788, Captain Arthur Phillip introduced prickly pears to Australia. He wanted to start a cochineal industry. Prickly pears grew so well in Australia that they escaped into the wild and are now a weed. Cochineal is still used in the dye industry. The dye is used to color makeup, such as lipsticks. It is also used to color foods, such as strawberry syrup.

Female cochineal scale insects are farmed. The insects feed on prickly pears.

Man crushing dried cochineal insects

The Eagle, the Snake, and the Prickly Pear

A Traditional Aztec Tale

Long ago, ancient Aztecs worshipped many gods and goddesses. To keep these gods happy, the Aztecs offered human **sacrifices**. Often the people they sacrificed had been captured from neighboring tribes. So the neighboring tribes feared and despised the Aztecs. Whenever the Aztecs tried to build a city, other tribes in the area would chase them away.

Finally, the Aztecs became desperate to build a city of their own. A powerful god spoke to them. He promised the Aztecs that they could have a great city, but it had to be in exactly the right place. To find that place, the people must look for an eagle perched on a cactus and holding a snake in its beak. When they found this place, they would have to stop waging war until the marvelous city was built.

For the next 200 years, the Aztecs roamed Mexico. They looked for an eagle perched on a cactus, holding a snake in its beak. One morning, a priest was standing on the shore of a lake, looking at a small island. He spotted an eagle perched on a cactus. A snake was writhing in its beak. The Aztecs were home at last! The Aztec people built a great city there. They named it Tenochtitlán (*Teh noach teet LAN*). This means "the place of the prickly pear." Today, it is the site of Mexico City.

Some words such as *god* and *goddess* indicate gender (male or female). The words *actor* and *actress* are another example. More and more, words that are gender neutral (neither male nor female) are being used. Some examples include: *spokesperson* and *firefighter*.

Mexico's coat of arms features an eagle perched on a cactus, with a snake in its beak. This emblem can be seen on the flag of Mexico.

SHOCKER

To please their gods, the ancient Aztecs would sometimes drive cactus spines through their tongues and other body parts until they dripped blood!

Did you know that digging up even a tiny cactus from the desert could get you into deep trouble? An area of land in Arizona's Sonoran Desert is due to be bulldozed so that new houses can be built there. Unfortunately, the area is home to the Pima pineapple cactus. In 1993, the government declared this little cactus to be at risk of extinction.

Sonoran Desert

WHAT DO YOU THINK?

Are conservation banks a good idea? Should people be allowed to destroy some cactuses if they pay money to save others?

PRO

Towns and cities are always going to spread, because people need places to live. Unfortunately, some plants will get harmed. So conservation banks are a good idea. Both sides are happy. The developers can still build, and the endangered species can be protected in specific conservation areas.

Now environmentalists and developers are discussing a plan to allow some of the plants to be destroyed in exchange for setting up conservation areas elsewhere. Developers who destroy cactuses to build houses will pay money to a conservation bank. This money will be used to take care of the cactuses in the protected conservation areas.

CON

If some cactuses are rare, they should not be harmed in any way. If not enough Pima pineapple cactuses are saved, they will become extinct. Letting people pay money for the right to destroy something sends the wrong message.

GLOSSARY

arid (*A rid*) very dry, usually because of lack of rain

arthritis (*ar THRYE tiss*) a condition that makes a person's joints swollen and painful

cell a basic part of a plant or an animal, so small it can be seen only with a microscope

cochineal (*KO chih nee uhl*) a red coloring used for food and dyes. It is made from the dried female of a kind of scale insect.

condense to change from a gas, or vapor, into a liquid

diabetes (*dye uh BEE teez*) a disease in which there is too much sugar in the blood

endangered close to becoming extinct

epiphyte (*EHP uh fite*) a rootless plant that grows on another plant, usually without harming it

evaporate (*ee VAP uh rate*) to change from a liquid into a vapor, or gas

noble (*NOH buhl*) a person born into a position of high social status, and often wealth

pollination (*pol uh NAY shun*) the transfer of pollen from one plant to another plant of the same species, enabling the second plant to reproduce

sacrifice an offering of something to a god or gods

toxic (*TOK sik*) poisonous

Victorian (*Vik TOR ree uhn*) the time of the reign of Queen Victoria of England (1837–1901)

Epiphytes

FIND OUT MORE

BOOKS

Gaff, Jackie. *I Wonder Why the Sahara Is Cold at Night and Other Questions About Deserts*. Kingfisher, 2004.

Goodman, Susan E. *Seeds, Stems, and Stamens: The Ways Plants Fit Into Their World*. Millbrook Press, 2001.

Hall, Margaret. *Venom and Visions: Art of the Southwest*. Scholastic Inc., 2008.

MacQuitty, Miranda. *Desert*. DK Eyewitness Books, 2000.

Murray, Peter. *Cactus*. Child's World, 1996.

Storad, Conrad J. *Saguaro Cactus*. Lerner Publications, 1994.

WEB SITES

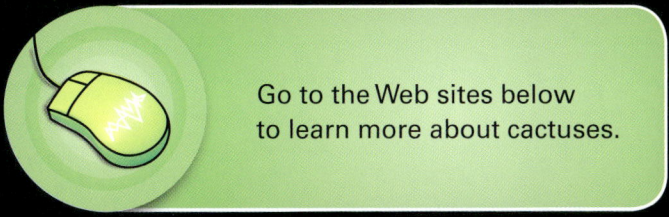

Go to the Web sites below to learn more about cactuses.

www.desertmuseum.org/visit/exhibits_cactusgardens.html

www.enchantedlearning.com/subjects/plants/types/cactus

www.desertusa.com/july96/du_saguaro.html

www.101kidz.com/activities/cactus/about.html

www.bbc.co.uk/gardening/gardening_with_children/didyouknow_cacti.shtml

INDEX

ABOUT THE AUTHOR

Yvonne Morrison finds cactuses fascinating. She loves their different colors and shapes. She has a huge backyard and plans to make a cactus garden one day. Yvonne lives with her husband in an old-fashioned cottage in a sunny seaside town in New Zealand. Her hobbies are dancing, listening to music, collecting antiques, and reading.